A WOMAN OF EXCELLENCE

Also by Sheri Powell

Pausing With God: A Journey Through Menopause (English)

Pausing With God: A Journey Through Menopause (Spanish)

Pausing With God: A Shut In Experience

A Woman of *Excellence*

THE MINISTRY OF MY MOTHER
a memoir

SHERI POWELL

SLP COMPANY
Sharing the Lord with People

A Woman of Excellence: The Ministry of My Mother
Copyright © 2019 by Sheri Powell

This book has been written as an instrument of encouragement for mothers and daughters everywhere. Never forget that you were created with and for a purpose!

Unless otherwise indicated, all scripture quotations are taken from the KJV/Amplified Parallel Bible, Zondervan Publishing House. All Rights Reserved. The Living Bible Copyright ©1971. Used by permission of Tyndale House Publishers, Inc., Wheaton, Illinois 60189. All Rights Reserved.

The Holy Bible, English Standard Version Copyright © 2001 by Crossway Bibles, a division of Good News Publishers.

All Rights Reserved. No part of this book may be reproduced in any form, stored in a retrieval system, or transmitted in any form by any means-electronic, mechanical, photocopy, recording, scanning, or other-except for brief quotations in critical reviews or articles, without permission in writing from the author.

Cover design by: Christine Dupre (Vida Graphic Design)
Edited by: Barbara Hollace (www.barbarahollace.com)
Interior design by: Russel Davis (Gray Dog Press)
Author photo taken by: Amy Ploss-Sampson (www.Figure8Studio.co)
Published by SLP Company, P. O. Box 9172, Fleming Isle, FL 32006
Printed by: Amazon.com/CreateSpace

Library of Congress Control Number: 2019901719
ISBN: 978-0-578-43246-5

When you PAUSE, visit our website: www.PausingWithGod.com
You can contact SLP Company or Sheri Powell at:

Email: PausingWithGod@gmail.com
Or write us at: Pausing With God Ministries, Inc.
C/O Sheri Powell
P. O. Box 9172
Fleming Isle, FL 32006

Printed in the United States of America
First Printing: 05/2019

DEDICATION

This book is dedicated to my mother,
DeLorise (Toots) Simmons

You are among one of the precious gifts
God has given us.

Thank you for teaching me that
being a mother is more than a title,
it is a ministry.

Sheri,
You are the author of your own life.
It's up to you to dream it, imagine it, sketch it, shape it,
build it, go after it, and make it happen.

And then color it in with bright, shining shades of joy and deep,
lasting shades of meaning that are yours and yours alone.
No one else can know the dreams you dream
or the strengths you have within you
that will help you make your dreams come true.

No one else needs to.
Because they're yours.
And so is today!

Love, Mom

CONTENTS

Foreword ix
Introduction xi

The Storm 1
None Given 5
Do You Know Her? 13
What About You? 17
These Three Words 25
Restoration 29
It Is Finished 37

Afterword 41
Epilogue 48
Bibliography 51
About DeLorise 54
About the Author 55

FOREWORD

As it should be with any of us who journey through life with integrity and humility, there ought to come a time when we acknowledge the deposits that others have made into our lives. In her latest publication, *A Woman of Excellence: The Ministry of My Mother*, our dear friend, Sheri Powell, seizes the opportunity to give honor to whom honor is due as she pays homage to her own mother.

True to her expressed desire to engage, encourage, and empower women, Sheri Powell reflects upon the transferable lessons she learned through her own upbringing. Her mother's ability to transcend the challenges of her life to become a powerful, proven force of love and grace become the substance of significant lessons for every woman.

We met Sheri approximately 25 years ago as a member of the church we pastored. At the time, she was a newly divorced mom doing a phenomenal job raising her young son and daughter. Since that time, she has moved out of state and remarried, adding a husband with three additional children to her household. The years have passed, the kids have all grown up, and a brand-new generation has been added to Sheri's family tree. God has been good to Sheri. She has grown in wisdom and experiential knowledge.

In this, her third publication, you will learn from two generations of excellent women. Enjoy the journey.

Pastors (Emeritus) Todd and Leslie Foster
Church on the Rock – New Haven, CT

INTRODUCTION

A mother's love has an enormous effect on a child's development. UCLA professor and psychiatrist Allan Schore, Ph.D., wrote in his book, *Affect Regulation and the Origin of the Self,* "The child's first relationship, the one with the mother, acts as a template, as it permanently molds the individual's capacities to enter into all later emotional relationships."

The transition to becoming a parent is challenging. As a result, with no template to refer to, though not impossible, it may be hard for a mom to love and care for her child. When I began penning this book, I was reacquainted with some memories from my past. They were not good ones, but unpleasant encounters with my mom. I wrestled for days before going any further, trying to decide if they should be included or not.

During this awkward interlude, I read an article titled, "Parenting 101: Everyone is Doing the Best They Can." It stated how it's easy to criticize, yell, berate, humiliate, etc. when there is a display of foolish, inappropriate behavior or when we fail to meet one another's expectations. I saw how this not only applied to my mom, but me as well. The purpose of this memoir would not be attained if I were to use this venue to place the blame or find fault with my mom. Having said that, please understand this will not be a "bashing my mom" kind of book. My intent is to share with you how the ministry of my mother brought me unspeakable healing. This book is to encourage you in all relationships, but especially those of a mother and daughter and vice versa.

A mother and daughter relationship has many facets and it takes a lot of effort to maintain a healthy one. There is a depth of vulnerability that resides within each of us. I do not know the current status of your relationship(s). Perhaps you are presently working through some challenges or perchance you are grieving the loss of your parent or your daughter. Or maybe your relationship with your mom is in a good place – that's wonderful news. Whichever the case may be, I am filled with expectation and anticipation that when you close the cover of this book you will be inspired at some level, be it in your present or future relationships.

There were three of us. I was born in the middle of two brothers. But our mom and younger brother had a relationship that was like none other. It didn't bother me that they had a connection that was so much more than a mother – son relationship, they were friends. Though a pain in her rear, my younger sibling was great company for her and she was his confidant.

My brother, Ronald Simmons, was tasked with introducing her to you, but regrettably he vacated his earthly vessel before this manuscript could be completed.

As I pause to think of him, I can hear his voice and the following is a snippet of what I believe he would say.

She was my buddy, my best friend, who wasn't just beautiful on the outside, her beauty shone from within. Whether in sweats or a dress, she was an unashamed classy lady with a magnetic personality. She loved people and people loved to be in her midst. She took pleasure in celebrating my accomplishments, no matter how big or small, and had the gift of creating teachable moments in the midst of my bloopers and blunders. Together we created so many memories, they will last us a lifetime. It is an honor to introduce to you, DeLorise Simmons – A Woman of Excellence.

A Woman of
Excellence

Chapter One

THE STORM

"Why go home? Wouldn't it be safer to go in the opposite direction of the storm?" Just as the ticket agent finished her sentence, I noticed an elderly couple gazing at one another with worried looks on their faces. I shrugged my shoulders. Glancing at my husband I whispered, "This sure is a funny way to end our vacation!"

Our conversation was interrupted by a computer-generated announcement. "We are sorry about the inconvenience. Due to inclement weather, several airports will be closing early. Please check local news and airport display boards for more information."

The gate attendants began scurrying from one side of their desk to the other, as the last plane headed to Florida taxied to the gate. As soon as the plane was in view from the window pane, everyone rushed to gather their belongings. The agent sternly spoke through the intercom system. "Ladies and gentlemen, in an attempt to make it to your destination ahead of the impending storm, the quicker you get on and seated, the sooner the plane can depart."

We swiftly moved past the flight attendants as they prepped for their safety demonstration. Squeezing into my seat, I buckled up and began wrestling with the tangled cord of my headphones. The plane began to roll down the runway, and with great haste, we were up, up, and away.

I turned my head, looked out the window, and whispered, "Lord, please bless us with a good flight." To ease my nerves, I turned on the in-flight entertainment, but so many thoughts were running through my mind. I found one of my favorite home make-over shows, and before long, I was sound asleep.

I was awakened by the voice of the captain over the intercom. "Welcome to Jacksonville International Airport." He continued speaking, sharing the baggage claim information, and gave his best wishes for those that would be in the path of the storm. From that point forward till we reached our car, everything was a blur. The memories of the previous week dissipated as the dark and puffy clouds in the sky captured our attention. As we exited the airport, our priority was to find a store and secure a few necessities.

We checked in with family and everyone was good, except our middle son. His home was in the flood zone and they had to evacuate. He and his family decided to come and hunker down with us. Arriving home first, we unpacked the car, but I couldn't separate myself from the doorway. It was like watching a tennis match, first staring at the sky and then the road. This went on until I saw their car come around the corner and pull into the driveway.

Everyone was dry, fed, and had found a place to settle in the family room. We took turns channel surfing, switching from one channel to the other comparing the latest weather forecast. Each meteorologist had their own interpretation on the anticipated direction, damage, and destruction of the storm.

It was hard trying to find some semblance of normalcy, while waiting to see what might happen next. To shed some of my anxiety, I

The Storm

peeled myself off the couch and quietly gathered flashlights and batteries and placed them in common areas throughout the house. Next on my list, wash clothes and take a hot shower.

A short time later, my mission was accomplished, and no one seemed to notice what I was up to. Feeling somewhat at ease, I decided to hang out upstairs until I heard a noise coming from below. The sound was familiar. I had heard it before but couldn't make it out, it was kind of muffled. I made my way across the room, pulling the bedroom door open, and made my way down the stairs. As my feet landed on the last step, at a snail's pace I slowly peeked around the corner. There they were, our middle son and his family, sitting on the floor so preoccupied that they didn't even notice me.

I studied the show on the television screen and then looked back at their expressions. Even though I couldn't figure out what was so humorous, their laughter was contagious. I chuckled for a second having no idea what I was laughing about. Excusing myself, I stepped over them to find a place to sit on the couch. I hesitated but asked anyway, "What is the name of this show?"

"*Catfish*," they replied in unison.

Catfish is an American reality-based documentary television show about the truth and lies of online dating. On the Internet, a "catfish" is a person who creates fake personal profiles on social media sites using someone else's pictures and false biographical information to pretend to be someone other than themselves. These "catfish" usually intend to trick an unsuspecting person or persons into falling in love with them.

MTV and the *Catfish* producers, Schulman and Joseph, help people who are emotionally entangled with someone they have never met in real life. Each episode is an investigation into whether or not the other participant in the virtual relationship that has been going on for months, or even years, is legitimate or if they are, in fact, a "catfish."

Whether or not two people are totally lying to each other and it turns out to be a huge disaster, is only the first part of the story. The producers, as well as the viewers, want to know the "who, what, and the why." The basis of the show is that the person who has been dishonest feels bad and wants to come clean after they have deliberately set out to deceive, without giving any thought to the emotional or mental drama they may have caused.

Growing up in the IBM Selectric typewriter era, any new technology for Mom was a bit intimidating. I remember when she acquired her first cell phone and it took months teaching her how to use it. She was amused at how information was not only managed but how quickly it could be retrieved. We often joked that if Mom owned a computer, she would be a menace to society.

With the massive amount of data available at our fingertips, social media is a storm brewing on the horizon. There is a hidden and present danger oblivious to anyone in its path. In an instant, lives can be transformed by words, pictures, videos, and blogs. Day in, and day out, our privacy, security, and safety are being compromised and it is hard to forecast where, who, or when it will strike next. While we can't deny the benefits, the ability to reconnect and stay in touch with family and friends, the drawbacks continue to be a threat, especially when the end user engages with these platforms with harmful intent.

Chapter Two

NONE GIVEN

She only had to show up, and Mom's sun-like appearance had the ability to brighten up an entire room. Whether she sat down or moved from one end to the other, her warm and inviting spirit, reminiscent of a sunflower, followed her. Her outer beauty was apparent, and a bright and cheery disposition erupted from within.

But like anyone, there were seasons of Mom's life that could be described as disheartening. The winter seasons were challenging. There were flurries of illnesses and other unforeseen circumstances that had the potential to break her spirit.

There were many times when it looked as if Mom was about to give in. Then all of a sudden right before your eyes, she would spring forth. The summers were a mixture. Some days were filled with spurts of energy, and other days, especially after her dialysis treatment, Mom would fall prey to fatigue and anxiety. Nevertheless, with each setback, no matter how long it took, she dusted herself off, rose up, and pressed on.

Life is a mystery. The human being begins life as a single cell, formed when a father's sperm fertilizes the mother's egg. When impregnation is complete, and the nuclei of egg and sperm have combined, a new being comes into existence and is capable of further development. How could she miss someone she never knew? I guess you could say, she mourned the missing person that had a hand in creating her. Whether two people are committed to one another or not, the birth of a child nevertheless echoes Psalm 127:3 (ERV), "Children are a gift from the Lord."

I raised my head cautiously, my eyeglasses sat comfortably on the crown of my head. I squinted and looked at the clock on the wall - it was a little after twelve noon. There was a gurgling noise in the lower part of my stomach, it hinted that I was hungry, but I couldn't budge. As I sat on the floor, my eyesight was blinded by the sun making its way through the curtain. My limbs had gone numb from sitting so long. I grabbed both of my legs and adjusted my position. Pushing back from the stacks of paper that lay near my left thigh, I slid over toward the right side of the room, near the box labeled M-O-M.

There was a deafening silence that enveloped the room. The only sound I heard was my hand running over the top of the faded yellow box. Lowering my hand inside, I could feel my breathing become erratic, as memories of my mom began swirling in my head. I mumbled to myself, "Am I really ready for this?" What could be in this box? Whatever it was, the fact remained, she was gone.

"Ready, set, go," I said aloud, as I turned the box upside down. I heaved a sigh and got started. As I arranged the papers in date order, tears collected underneath my eye, making their way to my shirt. Though I needed tissue, I was determined not to move. Out of nowhere, negative memories raced through my mind. There were so many difficulties and challenges that our family endured. While I didn't want to make light of any of them, I needed to wake up to the reality of these passing thoughts. I shook my head from side to side and asked myself, "Is there a family on this earth that hasn't experienced their share of hardships?" I answered myself, "No, there isn't." I squashed my thoughts by recalling that the good times outweighed the bad.

There are some family traditions that may appear to be silly to some, but they are priceless to the beholder. When I was young, I looked forward to Friday nights; they were fun and exhausting at the same time. Shopping was my mother's passion. She had a gift for finding a bargain in a haystack. Even when she didn't have any money, Mom used to say, "It doesn't hurt anyone to go window shopping." Most Fridays after Mom got off work, my maternal grandmother would pick us up and the journey began. Destination: Boston Post Road in Milford, Connecticut. Our Friday night excursions began with shuffling through the clearance racks of our favorite clothing stores. Second stop, grocery shopping, and our final stop was usually grabbing something to eat.

Saturday's ritual seemed to run congruent from one generation to another. From my grandmother's home to my aunts' homes, this family custom was the same. We'd rise early and clean the house from top to bottom. Teamwork in full effect, everyone understood the sooner we were done, the faster we could get on with our day. After the last chore was done, the matriarch of that home to say "thank you" usually made her way to the kitchen and cooked something for everyone to eat.

At our house, Saturdays ran the same, but when we were done my brothers would escape outside, and for the next few hours, I had her all to myself. Most of the time we didn't have any plans, we just hung out together. Every so often, we'd watch a movie and fall asleep before it was over. I remember this one time, I happened to wake up first. With my eyes wide open I laid there, listening to her breathing. I heard her whimper and moan in her sleep. I glanced over at her face and noticed her expression. It was as if someone was hurting her.

At last, the papers were arranged in some semblance of order and placed in a stack. There were two pieces of parchment-type paper that stood out from amongst the pile. I stretched forward and grabbed them both. My first choice was the one whose color was the lightest. I compared them. The inscription on both said, Birth Certificate, but the information on one was different from the other. On one certificate the baby's name was Mary Jane, and on the other, DeLorise Simmons. Both contained the same date of birth, time, place, and mother's name. Both were filed on the same day, but the witnessed section contained unlike dates. As I examined them, I noticed one of the certificates had a red watermark "amended" and witnessed on August 31, 2004, 58 years after her birth.

I questioned, "Why would my mother have a birth certificate for a baby named Mary Jane?" In addition, why was her mom's name in the title space provided on the certificate? It took me a minute to figure this out, but as I looked closer at the document, I realized that Mary Jane was my mother. She was the baby born on that day. Shaking my head, I thought, "Why the name change? What was wrong with Mary Jane?"

Adam Alter, an Associate Professor of Marketing at New York University's Stern School of Business, stated in an article that we identify very strongly with our names and they are an important part of the baggage that we associate with ourselves.

Not sure why, but just out of curiosity, I looked up the amended name. Though it's spelled slightly different, the name DeLorise means "sorrow." The million-dollar question is, what was Mom thinking when she picked the name DeLorise? She couldn't have been privy to the meaning back then, right? I know it might not make sense, but I am trying to solve the mystery or find a reason. Did her name change echo sentiments of what she may have felt at that time in her life – sorrow?

In case I missed any pertinent information, I continued to review the documents. My eye moved to a place where there should have been a name. I noticed this spot was left blank on both the original and the amended copy. Another mystery lay before me, why would this field be left blank? I paused and thought of several possibilities. It could have been accidentally left off in the midst of the excitement of her birth. Maybe her father had to rush off for some reason or another. These reasons didn't satisfy why there were two words in the spot where his name was supposed to be: "None Given."

As I was shuffling through the pile of papers, the memories of a conversation with my mom started coming back to me. I still don't have all the pieces, but I am sure Mom shared the story with me about the possibility of having another father. As she got older, she did her best, numerous times, to reach out to him. Each time, there was no response. Mom was disappointed again and again.

I'm told in her mid-forties, when she was just about to give up hope, finally her birth father responded. Mom was unsure how quickly he might vanish, so at their first meeting, her questions were more like an interrogation. When he did get a chance to speak, he made it worse. His responses sounded more like excuses and justification for his behavior. Mom wanted, maybe she needed him to say, what she had been dreaming about for years but instead he brushed her off. Her father ignored the discussion about his responsibilities instead he portrayed himself as the victim. When he had nothing more to say, there was a moment of silence, and then a short exchange of the possibility of talking again soon.

Months later, when they did get to meet in person, the visit was just as superficial as the phone conversation. There was no heart-to-heart talk, and no honest reconciliation. After a few years of one disappointment after another, Mom decided that there was no need to continue pretending. She walked away, fully understanding that it takes two people to work at reconnecting and maintaining a relationship. Though she found him, her father was still absent. Her sorrow remained, and the void had "no name."

The phone rang, "He's gone." The low and gloomy voice on the other end had been crying. The sniffles accompanied every word she spoke.

"Who's gone?"

"My father is gone."

You could feel the sorrow in her voice. I thought about that day she laid upon her bed, whimpering and moaning while she slept. Farfetched I know, but was Mom dreaming of him, could it be that she tried to reach out to him while she napped, but he wouldn't respond?

The thought of the situation led me to think about the show, *Catfish*. If this show was around years ago, Mom could have reeled him in. But then again, that may not have been a cool way to meet an estranged parent. His death made it final and any possibility of a relationship would never come to pass.

Well-known American author James Baldwin is known for this quote, "Know from whence you came. If you know whence you came, there are absolutely no limitations to where you can go." This inspirational quote reminds us that our origin can be the very compass that charts the path to who we become.

Without loving yourself, it may be difficult to have a healthy relationship with anyone else. Feelings of insecurity and loneliness can erect emotional and mental walls. From the outside, there is the appearance that one has it all together, but often if we took a peek on the inside, we would find an emptiness that inhibits one's ability to truly love themselves and others.

There is so much information out there that is supposed to help you live a healthier and happier life. From controlling your emotions to how to have a healthy self-esteem, The 5 Day Healthy Self-Esteem Challenge, The 30-Day Challenge to Increase Your Self-Esteem, and numerous others are offered on the Internet. I won't doubt the success of any of these, but if one has suffered from years of lack of self-esteem, it's hard to fathom that we can capture and squash it in five days or 21 days. Thirty days is more realistic, but it depends on the individual. If those who have a healthy self-esteem, struggle from time to time, how much more of a challenge is it for those who continue to wrestle from day to day?

The most challenging time in our lives is to find ourselves amid the labels and expectations that others have placed upon us. It is unfortunate that we believe what others say about us, before we take the time to find out for ourselves. When we stop listening to the outside voices and start following what we know to be true, we will then begin to feel liberated – free.

For Mom, perhaps the blank spot on the left side of her birth certificate was a contributing factor to the barrenness in her soul. She lived in a desert-like place for so long, that she became accustomed to it. But one day Mom woke up and stepped out of her pit. It became obvious that once she identified the origin of her darkness and understood what it was trying to do to her, she was able to turn her life around. Mom stopped listening to the voices that were telling her who she couldn't be and what she couldn't do. She then began ministering to herself, she was a child of God, Psalm 82:6, and she could do all things through Christ Jesus who strengthened her, Philippians 4:13. As a result, Mom was liberated, she was free, and the woman of excellence began to emerge.

All of us have challenges and difficulties, but it is the love we have for ourselves and for one another that makes all the difference. The truth is we don't get to choose our family, but we can choose how we respond to them. We choose to forgive, to love.

Her beginning may not have been what she would have it to be, but Mom had an ending that said, "Well done, my good and faithful servant." Before she departed from her earthly body, it was clear that she had won the battle. Though her birth father was absent and nonexistent in her life, another dad stepped in. Theirs was a relationship like no other. He loved her with an unconditional love. He shared with her how His thoughts about her were not for evil, but for good, to bring her to an expected end.

Her vertical relationship with God enabled her to freely express His love, His forgiveness, and extend His mercy. Nothing was perfect and every now and again, she spent a few moments thinking of what could have been, but she no longer allowed it to define her. In spite of everything, it was His presence in Mom's life that made all the difference, and it was His strength that enabled her to be whom she was created to be.

Chapter Three

DO YOU KNOW HER?

How well do you know your mom? Can you name her favorite ice cream flavor? Do you know the name of the city where she was born? What's her favorite song? Did she have a pet, if so, what kind, and what was its name? Does she have a favorite color? What was her first job? Can you name three things she likes?

Going through Mom's belongings confirmed what a special lady she was. I knew she loved to write but I didn't know how much until I began reading her journals. She wrote about all of her children. Mom wrote about how proud she was. I will particularly treasure the prayers she penned when we were in challenging seasons ourselves.

One of my dearest memories is when I was going through a difficult time physically. I would write about my experiences in my journal. At least three times a week, I would call Mom and share my entries with her. Regardless of how many times I called her with the same subject matter, she never tired of listening to me. Around 1999, I found out that I was smack dab in the midst of menopause. I'm grateful to her; it was Mom who encouraged me to write my first book. She said, "Menopause is not a subject matter that's talked about a lot, women need to know they do not have to suffer in silence." I thought she was just pulling my leg, trying to make me feel better. But a few days after her passing, I had one of the most precious moments that I shall hold onto forever.

As I was going through her belongings, I found a birthday card that she never got to send me. I opened the card and it read:

"Sheri, You are the author of your own life, it's up to you to dream it, imagine it, sketch it, shape it, build it, go after it, and make it happen. And then color it in with bright, shining shades of joy and deep, lasting shades of meaning that are yours and yours alone. No one else can know the dreams you dream, or the strengths you have within you that will help you make your dreams come true. No one else needs to. Because they're yours, and so is today! Love, Mom."

As her illness progressed, our relationship continued to blossom. It's funny how the circumstances in life will wake you up to the reality of its brevity. All that had weighed Mom down for so long was gone. She didn't need a name in the blank space on the left side of her birth certificate, for her heavenly Father had signed His name on her heart.

I appreciate the woman I have come to know. Watching her grow was like observing a sunflower from a seedling to full maturity. As the Word of God settled in her heart, the little girl who had self-esteem and self-worth issues began to sprout. Her perspective about her past, present, and future changed. This transformation was noticeable to all around her, and Mom loved who she saw when she looked in the mirror. The latter part of Mom's life as an empty nester gave the impression that she was wilting, no doubt her age and illnesses contributed to it. But she didn't let that stop her; Mom was resilient and always sought opportunities to help others.

I have been given a priceless inheritance to have watched Mom's journey, one that wasn't easy. But she showed us over and over again, that it's okay to fall, just don't stay down. I had a short forty-five years with her, but a lifetime of memories. Woman of excellence, I thank you!

Do You Know Her?

Here's a little fun exercise for you moms and daughters to see how well you know one another or a chance to get to know one another better. The following questions can be two-fold: moms, ask your daughters, and then daughters, ask your moms.

Might I suggest that you be sensitive and use wisdom. Be sure you have allotted enough time for this to be completed without any pressure or interruptions. Select a time when it's just the two of you, maybe go out to eat, go to a park and have a picnic or over a cup of coffee. Most of all – have fun with it!

For those whose mother may not be available, find a relative, a sister, cousin, or even close friend. If you are still unable to locate someone that can do this exercise with you, email me at PausingWithGod@gmail.com. In the subject line of the email write: *Mother & Daughter Do You Know Questions*, and we can complete the questionnaire together.

Do You Know?

Mother to Daughter

Mom's favorite color is
Mom's shoe size is
Mom's favorite flower is
Mom is how many years old
Mom's favorite thing to do is
Mom's favorite song is
Mom was born in which state/city
Mom has how many siblings
Mom's favorite dessert is
Mom is how tall
Mom's favorite beverage is
Mom, are her ears pierced

Daughter to Mother

Daughter's favorite color is
Daughter's favorite meal that Mom cooks is
Daughter's favorite book is
Daughter's favorite movie is
Daughter's favorite song is
Daughter's favorite school subject is
Daughter's favorite vacation ever was
Daughter wants to be when she grows up
Daughter's favorite beverage is
Daughter's favorite gift ever was
Daughter's favorite birthday ever was
Daughter's favorite thing to do is

Chapter Four

WHAT ABOUT YOU?

There are countless books turned into films whose storyline could be based on actual events. Books as well as the movie industry can often play a huge part in encouraging, educating, and enriching our lives. One of my favorites is *The Shack*. I read the book and watched the movie at least a dozen times since its release in March of 2017. I believe that movies like *The Shack* can be a tool that enables us to find strength in the midst of our struggles, and hope in the midst of our sorrows. When you close the cover of the book or leave the theatre, hopefully you get a sense that you are not alone. Perhaps there will be an awareness that others are going through similar or comparable situations.

The lead character, Mack, short for Mackenzie, and his mother grew up in an abusive home. Though the years of abuse took a toll on him, he grew up, got married, and had a few children of his own. From the outside you wouldn't think that his past had any effect on him, but what no one knew is that he suffered in silence.

His family started a tradition where they would go on an annual camping trip. This particular year his wife did not accompany them, it was just Mack and the kids. This excursion brought an unfortunate tragedy in his family's life. The last day of their camping trip his youngest daughter was kidnapped and murdered. Though tragic, this event opened a door of opportunity for Mack to genuinely get to know himself and come to a point where he could forgive his abusive father.

From generation to generation, each of us has been exposed to good and bad influences, attitudes, habits, and behaviors that we didn't realize we were exhibiting in our own lives. Not to make light of any of this, but you and I are not the first ones to come from imperfect descendants. There are numerous folks mentioned in the Bible that experienced dysfunction in their families. In Genesis, chapters 25-33, we see the family dynamic between twin brothers, Jacob and Esau.

Before they were born, their mother knew that these boys were going to be a force to be reckoned with. Rebekah, who had been barren for almost two decades in her marriage to Isaac, finally became pregnant. The babies struggled within her womb, making her pregnancy difficult. She was perplexed, and asked God why this was happening. His response went like this, "Two nations are in your womb, and two peoples from within you will be separated; one will be stronger than the other, and the older will serve the younger."

When it was time to give birth, Esau exited their mother's womb first. Jacob, known as the deceiver, followed holding onto his brother's heel. As they grew, these twins developed two different types of dispositions. Esau, an outdoorsy kind of guy, was their father's favorite. He was carefree and lived in the moment, without considering the consequences of his actions. Jacob, a homebody, was their mother's favorite. He was the quiet one and stayed close to home.

Throughout their childhood, the twins fought constantly for their place in their parents' hearts and position in their family. It was customary for the eldest brother to receive the blessing. Knowing he was near death, their father Isaac wanted to bless Esau before his eyesight became too bad. Rebekah, their mother, knew what Isaac was about to do, and because Jacob was her favorite, she used trickery to deceive her husband. She concocted a plan for Jacob to receive the blessing instead of his brother. When Esau found out what happened, he was beside himself with hatred for Jacob. He vowed that once their father died, Jacob had better run for his life.

Rebekah, who played a big part in Esau's dislike of his brother, wasn't about to take any chances of having her favorite son killed. She ignored the role she played and failed to address the real reason why Esau was angry in the first place. Aware of Esau's plans, she sought to manipulate her husband yet again. Rebekah plotted for Jacob to go away and live with her brother until Esau's anger subsided. The problem was that she had to convince Isaac that sending Jacob away was his idea.

She came up with a marriage proposition for Jacob. The prospects were slim in their surrounding community and she didn't want Jacob marrying any of the women who lived there. Rebekah presented Isaac with the suggestion that there was a better selection of wives where her brother Laban lived. It didn't take long before Isaac was convinced. He summoned Jacob, shared his concerns and gave him instructions, his blessing, and sent him on his way. When Esau found out about his brother's departure, he wasn't happy. He rebelled and married a woman from the very tribe his parents had instructed him not to marry.

In the meantime, Jacob made his way to his uncle's house. En route he met some shepherds and a young lady who happened to be his cousin. Her name was Rachel. Little did he know, she was his uncle Laban's youngest daughter. With one look at her, Jacob was smitten, and ran up to her and kissed the girl. Without saying a word, Rachel immediately ran home to tell her father all that had happened. Soon after, Jacob arrived at their home and her father Laban welcomed him into the family.

After being with his uncle for a month, Laban informed Jacob that just because they were related, it didn't mean he should work for nothing. He insisted that he pay Jacob for his labor. But Jacob presented him with a surprise proposal. He suggested that his pay would be to have Rachel, Laban's youngest daughter's hand in marriage. In spite of the custom practiced in their country that the youngest daughter cannot marry ahead of the firstborn, Laban gave permission for Rachel to marry Jacob.

Seven years passed, Jacob was excited that he was about to marry the love of his life. The following morning after the wedding, Jacob realized something wasn't quite right. The woman he thought he had married was not the woman that lay next to him in bed. His bride that said, "I do" at the altar, wasn't Rachel after all but her oldest sister, Leah. It became obvious to Jacob, that the deceiver was now the one who had been deceived. In spite of what transpired, Jacob still wanted Rachel, the woman of his dreams. He and Laban agreed Jacob would work another seven years for her hand in marriage.

There are some who might think that Jacob got what he deserved, but that isn't the reason why I shared his story. His misfortune sheds light on how the seeds of lies, deception, and manipulation can influence our lives and those of future generations. What about you? Maybe you have participated in a similar type of behavior like Jacob, or that of his mother, feeling like your back was against the wall. Or perhaps you've been on the receiving end and have been affected in some fashion. Regardless of which end you were on, the aftermath of the one betrayed or the betrayer can produce a tsunami effect on everyone connected to us.

Now let's fast forward to where Jacob had worked another seven years and was finally able to marry Leah's younger sister, Rachel. In addition to the two wives, Jacob had accumulated their handmaidens and fathered twelve sons and one daughter. It wasn't until after Rachel gave birth to his favorite son, Joseph, that Jacob asked his father-in-law to allow him to return to his homeland. Laban knew that he was blessed because Jacob resided in his household. In an attempt to detain him, Laban made another deal with Jacob, this time concerning the flocks. Even though Jacob noticed Laban's attitude toward him was not as it was before, he completed the business at hand before packing up his family and setting out to return home.

Jacob left, and on his way, the angels of God met him. After their encounter, Jacob felt compelled to reach out to his brother, Esau. He sent messengers ahead to let Esau know what he had been doing since Jacob left their native country. The messengers returned saying, "Esau is coming your way." Hearing this, Jacob became a little shaken as he was informed that Esau was not alone but had four hundred men with him. Not knowing what else to do, he separated his family into groups and he began to pray. During prayer, Jacob reminded God of the promises He made to him.

Despite prayer and his encounter with God, Jacob was still afraid. Spending the night in camp all alone, he selected the best from his flock. The gifts were separated into three caravans and placed in his servant's care. Each group would be sent ahead of him with a message for Esau. Jacob then took the remainder of his possessions and his closest family members and crossed the ford of the Jabbok. Known as a place of total surrender, in Hebrew, Jabbok means "to empty itself." After ensuring his family was safe on the opposite side, Jacob was all alone and began to wrestle with a man. The two toiled all night long. As day was breaking the man told Jacob to let him go. Persistent, he held on, even after the man knocked his hip out of joint.

"Let me go, for it is daybreak." But Jacob replied, "I will not let you go unless you bless me." The man asked him, "What is your name?" "Jacob," he answered. Then the man said, "Your name will no longer be Jacob, but Israel, because you have struggled with God and with humans and have overcome." Jacob said, "Please tell me your name." But he replied, "Why do you ask my name?" Jacob received his blessing and the conversation ended. Jacob was amazed! He had a new name (Israel) and had seen God face to face. Now he was seeing his life from a different perspective. Jacob had spent the majority of his life fighting. Actually, even in his mother's womb, he was seen wrestling. He clashed with his brother and his uncle Laban. Now at Jabbok, Jacob found himself in a fight with God. Here the deceiver was given an opportunity to surrender, to experience a new way of living.

The next day, Jacob looked up and there was Esau. He quickly divided up his family and went ahead of everyone to meet his older brother. Esau ran up to him, threw his arms around his neck, and embraced Jacob. As Esau kissed him, they both began to cry. As soon as they were done comforting one another, Jacob introduced Esau to his family. After the introductions, Esau couldn't wait to discuss the gifts that Jacob had sent to him. He expressed that he had plenty and there was no need to give him anything. Nevertheless, Jacob was so persistent that Esau had to agree to keep it all.

After the two kissed and made up, Esau was ready to move on and told Jacob, "Let's be on our way. I'll follow you." But Jacob had other plans. He suggested that Esau and his men go ahead of him. Jacob explained that he, his family, and his flock had come a long way, and he wanted to move them at a slower pace. Esau appeared to understand, yet he went on to propose that some of his men should remain with Jacob. Jacob declined his offer. He convinced Esau that they would be okay, and quickly changed the subject by expressing how grateful he was to be reconciled with his family.

There are relationships, like Jacob and Esau's, where there has been forgiveness but living in close proximity of one another does not take place, even after reconciliation. Jacob and Esau kissed and made up, but almost immediately after their reunion they separated again. Esau went one way and Jacob went in another direction. They forgave one another, or at least they gave the appearance that they did, and moved on with their families. The next time they would meet would be to bury their father Isaac.

What about you, can you relate to Jacob and Esau's story? The wrestling within Jacob was really with the man in the mirror. It doesn't matter if you are the one who has been betrayed or the betrayer, crossing Jabbok is necessary for everyone. Even in those severed relationships, where you don't know if there is any possibility of reconciliation, God will, if you avail yourself, remove the fear or any anxiety so you can walk in forgiveness.

What is important in any relationship is that we do not allow our experiences, situations, or circumstances to paralyze us from moving forward. Yes, it is easier said than done. It is a process, one without an estimated time of arrival but it is in our surrender that we get a clearer picture of who we were, who we are, and who God has created us to be. At Jabbok, we stop wrestling. We stop fighting, and are emptied out, so that we are able to receive. It is here that we let go of the past and hold onto God until He heals, comforts, restores, instructs, leads, and blesses us.

Chapter Five

THESE THREE WORDS

There are a lot of traditions that are passed down from one generation to another that are worth preserving. I can't remember how old I was when I acquired my first one, but every Christmas I would get excited. They were better than a friend, and it was okay with me if it was the only gift I received. Even though there were several presents under the tree, this was the first one that I looked for.

As I removed the gift wrap, I daydreamed and imagined what type of design would be on the cover. What about the line spacing? Was it "wide ruled or college ruled?" Once all the wrapping was off, at a snail's pace I pulled it toward my chest and whispered, "Hello, my friend." Resting in my hands, it appeared to be about five inches wide and seven inches long. This one had come with a key. I'd often chuckle when I saw this useless soft metal accessory. Access to my world could be granted with a simple hairpin or any sharp pointed object.

The sparkle from the gold writing on the cover blinded me. Nonetheless, I could still see the words, "My Diary." It was mine, a place to lay my thoughts, my dreams, and my aspirations. I assume that this recurring gift selection may have been because both of my parents journaled, and somehow, they decided to pass this tradition down to me. And as I became a mother myself, it was funny how I did the same for my daughters.

I picked up the green one. Seems like I had read this one before, but for some reason the words had a different effect on me. Mom's thoughts brought tears to my eyes. The words inscribed touched me as if I was reading them for the first time. Journaling can be used to personally organize one's thoughts and feelings. Her writings gave me the ability to understand her better; I was able to get a clear-cut picture of what was stored up in her heart.

Her journals were like a personal tutor. It wasn't about the quantity of the entry; it was the quality that moved me. The brief entries were just as important as the lengthier ones. She recorded memorable events, her heartbreaks, her disappointments, the prayers that led to some of her decision making, and a list of how to achieve her future goals. I felt blessed to be able to go back and read the changes and transformations that I'd seen with my own eyes. I could see how chronicling her thoughts conveyed clarity and also healing in various seasons of her life. I get it. I understand how far she had come and how hard she worked to get there. I admired her tenacity. Her entries reminded me that I may not be where I need to be, but every day that we are in the land of the living, we can thank God for another chance to make the necessary changes.

There was a common phrase that was repeated throughout her journals, three words to be exact, words that seemed to make all the difference, "I love you." She got it. Mom knew that God loved her, and she wrote how she loved Him. She inscribed how she loved her family, and regardless of the trials and tribulations that she endured, Mom was now comfortable in her skin, she unapologetically loved herself and the woman she had become.

While neither time nor the pages of this book would allow me to share all of her transcripts. I think she wouldn't mind if I gave you a glimpse of her past, present, and future. Here are a few remarks, dated from 1991 to the last few years of her life.

Why I Want To Be Saved

I want to be saved so that I can one day see my Lord & Savior, Jesus Christ. God loved me so much that He gave His only begotten Son. God has saved my life many, many times for that I am thankful, I am blessed. I want to do His will and obey His commandments so that I can do His work whatever that may be. I believe that He in His own time will reveal what He wants me to do for His cause. I can endure with God by my side. I can do all things through Christ which strengthens me.

Crucifying The Old Man

I long to live my life the way it is meant to be lived in Christ. This means putting aside everything I used to do – changing my whole lifestyle. No longer living in sin – doing the things that God would have me do and being obedient to His commandments and to live in the Spirit.

I am leaning precariously but confidently upon the Holy Spirit to guide my thoughts, words, and actions. The old man that was within me before has died and I am in a "newness of life." I am growing outward and upward into a larger life for God. I am surrendering to His power and love. I know that He has a plan for me; and a whole life change is before me.

As I write this, satan is on his job of attacking me as I continuously strive to get closer to God, he sees the change in me and is not happy; still trying to conquer my flesh – but my salvation is very precious. Therefore, my focus is on the Lord and I have to stay prayed up in order to live for Jesus. Old man, I say to you – I will win the battle. May the God of peace equip me with everything to do His will.

What Grace Means To Me

Grace is unmerited love that God has given us. He has delivered my soul in peace from the battle that was against me and there were many. For this I am grateful, for the blessings He has given me. God is my refuge and my strength and His grace, mercy endureth forever.

God's grace, His mercy has created in me a clean heart and has renewed a right spirit within me and He did not give up on me when I was out there in the world. He by His grace has restored me and has delivered me – for this I am grateful, and I will serve Him for all the days of my life. God is a good God!

What Is The Source Of Our Faith?

God is the source of faith. Being saved is the source of my faith. Being a living sacrifice unto God. Living holy and doing the will of God. My faith has grown, heightened more positive in waiting on the Lord. I am not what I used to do, taking things in my hands doing what I thought I should. I have learned to be still and wait on the Lord. But giving it to God in prayer, and only when He speaks to me do I act on things as He tells me. Constantly continuing to be patient in tribulations, continually prayerful. Always staying connected to the Lord.

These are a few of Mom's entries. She is revealing just how much their relationship means to her – everything. She is sharing her experiences, so that we too, can hear those three words, "I love you." It is evident as you read them how her confidence wasn't in herself, but in God. Mom appreciated how He patiently waited for her over the years as she learned how to remain with Him on the mountain top, yet continued to hear His voice in the valley experiences. The valleys were the hardest. She had to be sure to lean on Him while maintaining good courage. Those three words kept her believing and having faith in Him. Through it all, He never left her. And all the way till the end, she never wanted to leave Him.

Chapter Six

RESTORATION

One of my favorite stories is about a woman and her two daughters-in-law. As I was reading the narrative of their story, I'd imagine what their wedding day was like. Repeating their vows and saying, "I do," I presume with stars in their eyes for one another, they were blinded to the reality of being intertwined into one another's family.

I'm speaking of Ruth and Naomi. Their story can be found in the Bible between Judges and 1 Samuel. The book of Ruth contains 2,039 words and is divided into four short chapters. Their brief story has been read, interpreted, and applied in several different ways, and though considered a brief one, we will find that there is a lot going on in three separate households.

When we get married, we take for granted that we will have many years before "death us do part" occurs. Imagine the conversations Naomi, her husband, their sons and wives had during their after-dinner talks as they made plans for the future and dreamed about growing old together.

But as life would have it, their lives took an unforeseen turn. Naomi and her daughters-in-law unexpectedly became widows. Naomi had to deal with not just one loss, but three losses with her husband and two sons. What were these three women going to do? Each having been married for a number of years was now left to take care of themselves.

The culture back in those days was one where if your husband passed away, and there were no remaining offspring to marry, one is given the option to return home to their family. Furthermore, Naomi spoke about being too old to have another husband or any more children. As she and her daughters-in-law were walking and talking, Orpah didn't take long to make up her mind and immediately returned home. Ruth, on the other hand, seemed to weigh her options carefully. She left her family to marry this man and planned to live in holy matrimony for a long time, but now in the prime of her life, she was a widow.

I'd imagine Ruth up all night writing by candlelight the pros and cons of what she should do. Should I go back home as Orpah did or remain with Naomi? Something influenced her to stay. Perhaps it was how Naomi lived a life of integrity, a way of life that Ruth yearned for herself. The text reveals that Ruth wasn't remaining with Naomi to get something from her. Ruth was prepared to go beyond the norm. She told Naomi, "Don't urge me to leave you or to turn back from you. Where you go, I will go, and where you stay, I will stay. Your people will be my people and your God my God. Where you die, I will die, and there I will be buried." After that speech, Naomi realized that Ruth was determined to go with her, so she ceased from pressing her to leave.

Ruth's faithfulness to her mother-in-law is an illustration that in spite of what we may be going through, there is hope. Ruth didn't follow her to be a burden; she accompanied her to be a blessing. Day after day, in the hot sun, she went out to glean in the fields to provide for them both, without complaining.

Because of the way Ruth carried herself, she was noticed by one of Naomi's family members. Boaz was his name and what a coincidence that he just happened to own the fields where she gleaned. Here was this beautiful handmaiden, someone he had never seen before. Boaz wanted to know more about her. The overseer of the field told him her name, and all that she had been through. Boaz was so in awe of her compassion for her mother-in-law that he made it his business to be kind-hearted toward Ruth. He not only gave her permission to glean in his field, he commanded that she would also be protected. As Ruth daily sought to provide for Naomi, Boaz ensured that Ruth was taken care of as well.

Restoration

No one could have guessed that things would have worked out this way. Ruth, in the midst of her sorrow, made a difficult choice and because of her obedience she was the beneficiary of an unthinkable future. The latter part of her life turned out greater than her former years, and Boaz, her redeemer, her restorer asked for her hand in marriage.

I lift up my eyes to the mountains- where does my help come from? My help comes from the Lord, the Maker of heaven and earth. He will not let my foot slip—He who watches over me will not slumber; indeed, He who watches over Israel will neither slumber nor sleep. The Lord watches over me—the Lord is my shade at my right hand; the sun will not harm me by day, nor the moon by night. The Lord will keep me from all harm—He will watch over my life; the Lord will watch over my coming and going both now and forevermore.

Psalm 121:1-8 is a portion of scripture that Mom would often recite, especially on those days when she couldn't get out of bed. Looking from the outside you didn't know how she kept moving. But on the inside, her confidence was in the same God that Ruth and Naomi served. She may not have suffered like them, but nevertheless Mom endured numerous losses.

For years, Mom had a specific prayer that she regularly brought to the Lord. She understood and took James 1:6 literally, "When you ask, you must believe and not doubt." He already knew, but she kept asking, she kept praying. It was dear to her heart that God would restore certain relationships within our family. From time to time Mom would mention that she was hopeful that it would happen while she was alive. Yet if it didn't, she stated that it was well with her soul if God chose to answer her prayers after she was gone.

For more than a year, Mom was shuffled from the hospital, to the rehab, to the nursing home facility almost in that order. There were several times when it didn't seem like she was going to make it. During these times the doctors would call a meeting and basically give us no hope, but Mom proved them wrong and bounced back each time. I remember when one doctor said she could no longer live by herself; this news shook her to the core. She'd expected as much, but to hear someone say it aloud, she was hard-pressed to face that reality.

Mom hadn't lived in her apartment for several months. As we digested the recent news from the doctors, there were many questions we needed to face and answer. Should she continue to pay rent? What would she do with her belongings? I tried to ease her mind and let her know that she could come live with us, but this didn't bring her any comfort. We all knew how hard she worked over the years to get her apartment just the way she wanted it. Mom was still in shock, so we waited for her to bring the subject up. A few days later, the opportunity presented itself cloaked in her sense of humor. She joked about how no one has a U-Haul truck following them with their stuff when they leave this earth.

Mom continued sharing about what a good life she had. She reminded me that none of us knows our last day on this earth and she was determined to live each day like it was her last. At first, I thought that statement sounded morbid, but the reality is, do you or I really know the day or the hour when we will take our last breath?

Mom told me she came to the realization that she probably wouldn't be going back home, and no longer wanted to pay rent for a place where she couldn't reside. She gave me instructions on whom to give what to. The list contained every piece of furniture.

That evening, alone in her apartment, although it may have been unoccupied for a season, it was not vacant of her scent. I walked around from the kitchen to the bedroom and found myself tearing up. I, too, had to accept the reality that Mom would not be coming back to this residence.

Shortly after Mom was given the news that she wouldn't be able to return home, she became silent and withdrawn. Communication between us was different and I didn't know what to do. In an attempt to cheer her up, I made a few phone calls to family members and suggested that we get together. Over the next few days, with no agenda, they began to pour in. I was grateful that those she hadn't seen in a while were able to make it. It was standing room only. Some sat, and others leaned against the walls in her room. We giggled and laughed so hard the nurse came down the hall to Mom's room. We thought she was going to ask us to leave, but instead requested that we close the door.

From the left to the right I scanned the area. All of a sudden, it dawned on me, her prayers were being answered. Right before my very eyes, relationships that had been strained over the years were being restored. Forgiveness, love, mercy, and grace were the fragrance in her room. You could feel a release from the past and a wonderful embrace of the future. All of this was happening because of Mom's prayers. Our family was being restored and our Redeemer was amongst us. I nodded in awe and thought this is what she had earnestly prayed for. That night when I laid my head on my pillow, I smiled, looked up where our help comes from, and thanked God for not just hearing, but for answering her prayers.

All of us have a season in our lives when things do not go the way we intended or planned. In these times we may fail to see what is going on right in front of us. Ruth, when she lost her husband, may have pondered a bit before committing to remain with Naomi, but she never lost focus of the God her mother-in-law served.

It's no different with us. Each one of us currently has a situation, trial, or circumstance where we need God to intervene. Perhaps it's in your relationship with your mother, daughter, or even mother-in-law. Is there a need for forgiveness or a situation where mercy and grace can be extended? I love the story of Ruth. It reminds us that what matters is that love wins! Even in the midst of losing her husband, Ruth didn't allow that to stand in her way or stop her from doing what she was called to do. It's the same for us, we have everything to gain. Christ, our Redeemer, who never sleeps or slumbers is still in the business of restoring lives.

There were some days where Mom was in a lot of pain. The nurse would come in and administer medication to help her get comfortable. Watching her drift off to sleep reminded me of those Saturday naps when I was a teenager. Without giving it a second thought, I pushed the high back chair up to her bed and laid my head by Mom's side.

I felt Mom stirring. Not wanting this moment to end, I didn't move to see what she was doing. Without looking, I could feel her staring at me, her eyes on the back of my head. I waited a few more minutes before I turned to look at her. No words were necessary. It was as if her eyes communicated directly to my heart. She didn't speak but lifted her hand and began to massage my head. Her hand started from the top of my forehead to the back of my neck. All the while no one said a word. The silence was almost frightening yet comforting at the same time.

After a while, we began to talk briefly. Mom shared that she wasn't sure where she would be without her faith in God. She spoke a few more words and then asked for some water. She slowly sipped a few times and then let the cup go in my hand. A few minutes later, we talked a little and then Mom communicated that she was ready to go; she was tired. At first, I thought she was ready to go back to sleep. But I realized what she meant, when she repeated that phrase. I held back the tears and mustered up a response, "I know, Mom."

Restoration

Before I could take in all of what she had just said, with a tone of authority, Mom instructed me to get a piece of paper and something to write with. Giving me every detail, she began to dictate her homegoing service. I wrote down every word from what she wanted to wear to who was to speak. It's hard to imagine, but we found ourselves laughing and then crying, then our crying turned into laughter. When Mom was finished, she stayed awake while I read my notes from the beginning to the end. It was important that I got everything down exactly as she said. Before I could utter the last sentence, she nodded, her eyes closed, and she fell asleep.

I laid the pen and pad to the side. I took this time to return my head to the bed. Our conversation left me numb, but the pattern of her breathing kept me optimistic. I could feel her hand returning to my head. It was warm as she touched me. I thought, even now, Mom knew as she always did, exactly what I needed. As she rubbed my head, she began to speak, sharing how proud she was to be my mother and thanked me for being her daughter. After a brief pause, Mom continued massaging my head, I just laid there silent, relishing every moment.

Chapter Seven

IT IS FINISHED

Mom knew what God had called her to do. Her physical condition didn't stop her. Her reliance on Him was steady, no matter what the report of the day was from the nurses and doctors. Mom said that God used everything that came her way to shape her. It was in her shaping that she learned to trust the Lord with all her heart, mind, and soul.

Mom had dialysis three times a week. Even though her body was twisted in pain, she would look around to see if others were in need. The recipients ranged from the CNAs, to the nurses, to other patients. This is how Mom had lived her life, not even illness could stop her generous ways. Whether a glass of lemonade or their favorite take-out food, she wanted them to know she cared. Mom sought to be a blessing, not a burden.

My mother wasn't a woman of excellence because she had all her t's crossed and i's dotted. It was because she stayed the course. This woman of excellence was a Titus and Proverbs 31 woman all wrapped up into one. She is the woman I will always remember – the mother, the confidant, the friend that I will always miss.

Today we celebrate a Woman of Excellence. DeLorise Simmons, Toots to some, Nana, Grams to others. My mother prepared her homegoing for us back in April of 2008. She expressed her desire with fearless anticipation as she made sure I had paper and pen in hand.

The Word of God says in Exodus 20:12: Honor thy father and thy mother: that thy days may be long upon the land which the Lord thy God giveth thee. In the New Testament, we see in Ephesians 6:1-3, Children, obey your parents in the Lord: for this is right. Honor thy father and mother, which is the first commandment with promise, That it may be well with thee, and thou mayest live long on the earth.

In the midst of my mother's illness I asked God why she had to suffer so. I found comfort as God reminded me that He too had a close relative that suffered, His name was Jesus.

John 6:40 ... And this is the will of him that sent me, that everyone which seeth the Son, and believeth on him, may have everlasting life: and I will raise him up at the last day.

God's ways are bigger than ours. He saw beyond Mom's illness and because she looked to Jesus and believed in Him, she has eternal life. Mom knew what God had called her to do, she was to pray without ceasing. It was prayer that restored her relationship with Jesus, restoration for our families and for those who were near and dear to her. Her faith was anchored in God and she relied on Him no matter the report of the day. Mom knew He was keeping her, and she communicated that God was using everything that she was going through to shape her. It was in her shaping that she was faced with the questions of, "How much did she trust God?" "Was she willing to give her life totally to Him?"

God has blessed us with a true champion. We have a lifetime of precious memories and endless lessons in Fashion 101. In her time of molding in the Potter's hands, she jotted down some thoughts that I shared in Chapter 5: I Want To Be Saved, Why I Want To Be Saved, What Grace Means To Me, and Crucifying The Old Man.

For sure, Mom, that is what you have done, your prayers and life have restored our family. I believe on November 4, 2008 Jesus said, "Well done, good and faithful servant; thou hast been faithful over a few things, I will make thee ruler over many things: enter thou into the joy of thy Lord." (Eulogy from Mom's homegoing service, December 15, 2008)

It Is Finished

It may be hard for most to understand this, but many years ago when Mom first rededicated her life to Christ, I had a specific request myself. I asked God to heal our mom. I didn't just pray for her physical healing, but for her to be emotionally, mentally, and spiritually whole. As she grew weaker physically, I witnessed her becoming stronger in Him. Her countenance became more radiant, she was content, not anxious about anything. I realized just like Mom's prayer that my prayer had been answered. She was whole. God had given her beauty for ashes, the oil of joy for all those years that she had mourned. Mom had become the planting of the Lord.

I am aware that my mom has passed the baton to me, but also to you. It is God's desire that every one of His daughters be encouraged, receive from Him so that each of us will become all we were created to be – Woman of Excellence. Here's the baton, it's your turn now!

AFTERWORD

I'd like to take a moment to share the provision and providence of God. For several years before moving to Florida in the summer of 1999, my family and I participated in a weekly outreach in several communities. When one of our outreach partners found out we were moving, he name-dropped and told us that we needed to hook up with this guy in Florida who had five different sites for the same weekly outreach we were currently doing.

I was so excited. After we moved and got settled, we sought out the gentleman and scheduled a meeting. During our conversation, we realized that all of his sites were in Jacksonville, so we decided to meet at the site that was the closest to us. It was located inside a local Boys & Girls Club on the west side of Jacksonville. For several weeks, we visited and watched. I'd leave the community amazed at what was taking place and the opportunity that had been presented to us.

We immediately joined in and made new friends and this community became our extended family. In addition to the weekly outreach, I was given an opportunity to mentor the young girls in this community. We learned that they didn't require much, they were simply looking for us to be consistent and people of our word. If we said we'd be back next week, they expected us to be back next week.

Over the next several months, a relationship formed, and we began to join them on different events, outings, and a life-changing week in Branson, Missouri at KAA (Kids Across America) summer camp. Over the next ten years, we had countless amazing experiences and so many stories to tell from volunteering at this site.

It was during one of the mentoring sessions with the young ladies that the Annual Mother & Daughter Prayer Breakfast was birthed. The girls would plan, practice, and prepare for months. They worked as a team to create a program full of surprises. The first year we made a continental breakfast using microwaves and toaster ovens. The next year, we added more microwaves and donated food. With each year, the participants along with the attendees increased. By the eighth and final year of hosting the breakfast, the Lord provided and allowed us to invite the whosoevers and we fed well over 200 people FREE of charge.

While I am not promoting social media, I will say that it has provided us with an opportunity to reconnect with several of the girls. They have families and careers and continue to be responsible and caring citizens. We are planning and prepping for a Mother & Daughter brunch where we can reunite with those who participated in the past as well as celebrating with new attendees.

Annual Mother Daughter Breakfast

When I think of what the mother/daughter breakfasts mean to me, I can say that it meant everything. I was only fourteen years old and I was privileged to witness the most beautiful testimonies come to life before me.

I have witnessed these miracles in my own life and I know it was because I was able to attend the Mother & Daughter breakfast. My eyes were opened to the amazing work that God does each and every day. God used women from all walks of life to show me that no matter how imperfect we may be He can still use us individually and collectively.

One of the best parts that I loved was the fact that my mother and I could spend a few hours together and praise the Lord, our Creator. Every year, I would look forward to the next one, more than I did my homecoming dance that freshman year of high school.

During the mother/daughter breakfast, I realized that the bond my mother and I have is absolutely God-driven. I am grateful that, to date, the bond has only grown stronger. Because of our vertical relationship with the Lord, we find ourselves learning more and more about one another each day.

The mother/daughter breakfast also allowed me to evaluate myself and where I wanted to be with God on a personal level. I know that no one can separate me from the love of Christ and He will continue to use whosoever is willing to touch the lives of others the same way we were renewed that day.

I know it was almost 14 years ago, but the experience has never left my soul and I use it with every day on this journey called life.

Jazmin Quiros

Growing up not sure why but most of our family members had nicknames. It's not like we didn't like the names. Now that we are adults, some of us don't want anyone to know the label that we grew up with. Except Aunt Toots, who I thought "Toots" was her real name. I was so young and took things in life for granted.

Unfortunately, we don't know how much we appreciated someone until they are no longer with us. I can say from my heart, I loved Aunt Toots. There is so much I would like to say, but I don't have the vocabulary to express exactly how I feel at this moment in time. I remember her sweet, gentle countenance (her youngest son Ronnie had the same qualities). The quiet way in which she carried herself left a lifetime impression on me, and for this, I am grateful!

Your niece, Priscilla

My Friend

I remember it like it was yesterday, our friendship began more than thirty years ago. Her younger sister Yvonne aka Vonnie married my cousin's cousin – so we were so-called "family." Vonnie opened a modest lingerie shop on Dixwell Avenue in New Haven, Connecticut. The shop would exhibit its merchandise by hosting shows and I was asked to model some of their apparel. Toots, ever the style icon, would come by and give her creative feedback and we gravitated toward one another the moment we met.

Our relationship developed further when I was hired by the State of Connecticut, the same office where Toots worked. With the challenges and constant changes of the job, I could always count on her insight and sense of humor to encourage me.

Throughout the years, she had some health issues, but observing from the outside, you'd never know it by looking at her. She had style. Toots was a class act, always perfectly turned out and polished. During the workweek, she had to get up *"at 5:30 a.m. to get herself together."* It took a lot to keep Toots together.

Before I retired, I took that conversation to heart and for twenty-five years I was up at the same time, getting myself "together" so that I could arrive at work at 7:00 a.m. Toots taught me that in spite of how you feel or what you may be going through, it is important to present your best self. She would often say, "There's no need to LOOK like you're going through it!"

Anybody that knew Toots knew she LOVED to shop. I must admit that I was her enabler, chauffeur, partner in crime, whatever you want to call it, and we did some damage over the years. Whenever a new place popped up on the shopping radar, we were ride and die girls.

We kept our favorite spots a secret. We wouldn't tell anyone. Every so often, she'd have these "flash sales" out of her closet, and boy, did I ever get some great deals! We'd plan Saturday trips to NYC or just to the mall in White Plains if we had a Monday holiday, shopping and lunching to our heart's content.

We'd established a Columbus Day tradition with another friend who shared Toots' birthday. We'd go up to her birthday twin's home in northwestern Connecticut, and from there we'd head up to an inn on Lake Waramaug in Litchfield County. After lunch, we'd do some leaf peeping and catching up with each other. I really miss those autumn afternoons in October.

When Toots retired, a bunch of us girls got together and took her out for a nice dinner at a secluded restaurant/inn outside of Norwalk. It was a fabulous evening and meal for a fabulous woman! She'd helped so many young women (clients and co-workers alike) over the years with housing, jobs, wedding plans – you name it. If it required common sense or a touch of class, Toots was the person whose advice you sought.

Toots was a truly creative and talented woman who would receive many inquiries for hire. She excelled in calligraphy, her handwriting was exquisite. Toots had an awesome eye for detail and decorating was her gifting, placing the right piece in the right place. Unfortunately, Toots was often taken advantage of as people wanted her gifts and talents. I'd frequently chastise her for letting people use her. She'd always say, "That's OK, they'll get theirs. I'm not going to worry about it."

Sometimes on Saturday evenings Toots would call me up for a "fashion consultation" as she called it, looking for my opinion on what she was contemplating wearing to church. I always thought it odd but counted it an honor that this DIVA was seeking my input! I mean, it's one thing to think you're sharp, it's something altogether different to KNOW you're sharp, and baby, Toots KNEW she was sharp! I still have some stuff in my closet that I bought from or with her. Like her, the classics stay classic...

I remember one Saturday afternoon we'd stopped for lunch after a morning of shopping and she drank two large iced teas before our meal came. I asked how she was feeling. Toots said she was really thirsty all the time. I told her she needed to get her blood sugar levels checked since extreme thirst was a symptom of diabetes. Not long after, she was diagnosed with type 2 diabetes.

Once I went by to visit her at home. She'd had a pretty rough year health-wise. Her cardiologist had recently called her and was astonished that she was "still alive" after a year [he'd treated her and said he always called clients a year later to check on them.] Toots was resilient and went on to beat the odds several more times after that.

The last time I saw her she was in rehab after a surgery. It was too brief a visit. Toots was telling me about another surgery that she might have to undergo. I remember apologizing to her for not coming to see her, but my own mother's health was failing and much of my free time was spent looking after Mom. I was very overwhelmed, working two jobs and taking care of my mom in between, and feeling guilty because my friend needed me to be a friend to her and I just couldn't. I write this with tears streaming down my face because it still hurts me. Toots told me she understood and that she was tired of being sick. I knew it must have been true, I could hear it in her voice.

Although she was about 15 years older than me, she never "auntied" or "big sistered" me – we were girlfriends - sharing laughs and secrets, hurts and joys, advice and warnings. A week after her homegoing service I had to put my mom in a nursing home, one of the hardest things I've ever had to do – so I never grieved my friend's passing. I prayed for her forgiveness and keep a picture of her on my desk to this day. Some people you just don't ever want to forget. I know she's getting the rest she deserves. Toots loved a good, red manicure, Design by Paul Sebastian perfume, high heels, and my mama's bread pudding. Actually, anybody's bread pudding!

Toots loved her children, grandchildren, and church family and often spoke of how good the people there were to her. But what I remember is how good she was to all of us. Love ya, Toots...Your sister, Willette Barnet

Afterword

July 19, 1983

To My Dear Daughter Sheri,

Do not be afraid. You are not alone, you are never without help. God is with you where you are. Right at this moment you are in the very presence of God.

Do not be afraid. You can meet and overcome every challenge. You can take the steps that are needed to bring you the results you so earnestly desire. God's light is shining steadily on your path, revealing the way of your highest good.

Do not be afraid. The fears for the moment are temporary. They vanish as you call on your faith. You can rise up and out of any kind of limitation. You can be free and well and happy. You can be all that you long to be.

Your Mother
Love Always

EPILOGUE

We never like to let an opportunity pass without encouraging you.

[10] Fear thou not; for I am with thee: be not dismayed; for I am thy God: I will strengthen thee; yea, I will help thee; yea, I will uphold thee with the right hand of my righteousness. [11] Behold, all they that were incensed against thee shall be ashamed and confounded: they shall be as nothing; and they that strive with thee shall perish. [12] Thou shalt seek them, and shalt not find them, even them that contended with thee: they that war against thee shall be as nothing, and as a thing of ought. [13] For I the Lord thy God will hold thy right hand, saying unto thee, Fear not; I will help thee. —Isaiah 41:10-13

You are His and He is yours. No matter what you have been through, what you may be experiencing or what is up ahead . . . God will never leave you.

Epilogue

If you've never asked Jesus to be your Savior, we'd like to provide you with an opportunity to do just that, it's as easy as ABC.

A – Admit

Admit honestly to God that you have fallen short of living the way He intended for you to live.
The Bible says in Romans 3:23:
All have sinned and fall short of the glory of God.

B – Believe

Believe that Jesus died on the cross, was buried, and rose again.
The Bible says in John 3:16:
For God so loved the world that He gave His only begotten Son, that whoever believes in Him should not perish but have everlasting life.

C – Call

Call upon on Jesus.
The Bible says in Romans 10:13:
Whoever calls on the name of the Lord shall be saved.

If you have repeated these ABCs:

1. Pick a book in the Bible and begin reading.

2. If you do not have a church home, find a Bible-believing church. Hebrews 10:25 reminds us to not neglect meeting together.

Congratulations and welcome to the family of God!

BIBLIOGRAPHY

— *Affect Regulation and the Origin of the Self*, Allan Schore, Ph.D., Christian Counseling, Revised and Updated Third Edition
— "Parenting 101: 'Everyone Is Doing the Best They Can.'" *Funderstanding Education Curriculum and Learning Resources*
— "Catfish." *Urban Dictionary*, www.urbandictionary.com/define. php?term=Catfish.
— "Catfish: The TV Show." *Wikipedia*, Wikimedia Foundation, 27 Nov. 2018, en.wikipedia.org/wiki/Catfish: The_TV_Show
— "The Dangers of Social Networking." *TurboFuture*, TurboFuture, turbofuture.com/internet/The-Dangers-of-Social-Networking-Why-you-need-to-be-careful
— "Hurricane Irma." *Wikipedia*, Wikimedia Foundation, 24 Nov. 2018, en.wikipedia.org/wiki/Hurricane Irma
— Dad, A. (2018). A Loving Dad, Missing You Poem. [online] Family Friend Poems. Available at: http://www.familyfriendpoems.com/poem/a-loving-dad [Accessed 5 Dec. 2018]
— "Divorce – What Girls Miss When Dad Leaves The Home." *Psych Central*. com, 8 Feb. 2013, blogs.psychcentral.com/family/2009/12/divorce-what-girls-miss-when-dad-leaves-the-home/
— Harmon, Katherine. "How Important Is Physical Contact with Your Infant?" *Scientific American*, 6 May 2010, www.scientificamerican.com/article/infant-touch/
— Washington, Debrina. "Pros and Cons of Listing a Father's Name on the Birth Certificate." *LiveAbout*, singleparents.about.com/od/custodyoptions/a/name-on-birth-certificate.htm
— "Dr. Phil's Advice for a Woman in a Custody Battle with Her Parents | Dr. Phil." Dr. Phil, 1 Dec. 2015, www.drphil.com/videos/dr-phils-advice-for-a-woman-in-a-custody-battle-with-her-parents/
— "The Future of Social Media: 3 Predictions for 2017." *Business 2 Community*
— "Amended." *Merriam-Webster*, www.merriam-webster.com/dictionary/amended
— "Delores." *Freddy Name Meaning*, 22 Aug. 2018, www.sheknows.com/baby-names/name/delores
— "Parental Liability Basics." *Findlaw*, family.findlaw.com/parental-rights-and-liability/parental-liability-basics.html
— Washington, Debrina. "Pros and Cons of Listing a Father's Name on the

- Birth Certificate." *LiveAbout*
- "The Future of Social Media: 3 Predictions for 2017." *Business 2 Community*
- "How Do You Affect Your Child?" *Developmental Psychology at Vanderbilt*, Vanderbilt University
- "How Does Technology Affect Family Communication?" Livestrong.com, Leaf Group
- "Unborn Children." Society for the Protection of Unborn Children, www.spuc.org.uk/abortion/human-development-of-the-unborn-child
- Taylor, Jim. "Is Technology Creating a Family Divide?" *Psychology Today*, Sussex Publishers
- "James Baldwin Quotes." Goodreads, www.goodreads.com/quotes/14373-know-from-whence-you-came-if-you-know-whence-you.
- "The Mother-Daughter Connection." *Family Education*, 20 Sept. 2007
- "Farming." *Wikipedia*, Wikimedia Foundation, 30 Nov. 2018
- Proflowers.com, www.proflowers.com/blog/history-and-meaning-of-sunflowers
- Wee, Tré "Relationships Are like Gardening; You Reap What You Sow." Medium.com, *Medium*, 3 Apr. 2017
- "The Shack (2017 Film)." *Wikipedia*, Wikimedia Foundation, 27 Oct. 2018
- *The Shack*. IMDb, IMDb.com, 1 Mar. 2017
- "4 Fun Ways to Get Baby to Talk." *Parenting*, 10 July 2014
- "Unborn Children." Society for the Protection of Unborn Children
- *The Sterilization Movement and Global Fertility in the Twentieth Century*, eBook: Ian R. Dowbiggin: Kindle Store
- "Parental Responsibility Laws In All 50 States | Matthiesen, Wickert & Lehrer, S.C. Reference Chart | Most States Have Parental Responsibility Laws That Hold Parents or Legal Guardians Responsible for Property Damage, Personal Injury, Theft, Shoplifting, and/or Vandalism Resulting from Their Children's Actions. This Chart Covers Parental Responsibility Laws for All 50 States." Matthiesen, Wickert & Lehrer S.C., www.mwl-law.com/resources/parental-responsibility-laws-50-states/
- "10 Ways Low Self-Esteem Affects Women in Relationships." *Psychology Today*, Sussex Publishers
- Kellgren, Samantha. "30-Day Challenge to Increase Your Self Esteem." Everyday Power Blog, 1 Oct. 2018
- "Do You Struggle With Self-Esteem? THIS Is For You..." *After the Affair - Infidelity Healing*, 8 Jan. 2018
- "BibleGateway." Acts 3:9-10 NIV - - Bible Gateway
- "BibleGateway." Psalm 127 ERV - - Bible Gateway
- "BibleGateway." Psalm 127:3 ERV - - Bible Gateway
- "BibleGateway." Luke 10:38 KJV - - Bible Gateway
- "BibleGateway." Genesis 25-33 KJV - - Bible Gateway
- "BibleGateway." James 1:6 KJV - - Bible Gateway
- "BibleGateway." Psalm 121 NIV - - Bible Gateway

Bibliography

— "BibleGateway." Proverbs 31:10 NIV - - Bible Gateway
— "Bible Gateway Passage: Ruth - King James Version". Bible Gateway
— "BibleGateway." Matthew 25:21 NIV - - Bible Gateway
— itsoverflowing.com, itsoverflowing.com/2011/09/overflowing
— Choyce III, Jonathan F. *"Tomorrow Isn't Promised"* used with permission
— *"The Importance Of Passing Down Family Traditions - Sunshine Retirement Living"*. Assisted Living & Independent Living For Seniors, 2018
— *"Children Learn What They Live -- Complete Version"*. Empowermentresources.com, 2018
— "Why Self-Help Books Rarely Work". *HuffPost*, 2018
— "Airport Check-In". En. Wikipedia.Org, 2018, https://en.wikipedia.org/wiki/Airport_check-in
— "How Can Weather Affect My Flight? | Privatefly Blog". Blog.Privatefly.Com, 2018
— "The Truth About Turbulence: What Passengers Should Know". The Points Guy, 2018
— "Types Of Emotions | Positive And Negative Types of Emotions List | The Emotions". The-Emotions.Com, 2018
— "Check-In". En.Wikipedia.Org, 2018, https://en.wikipedia.org/wiki/Check-in
— "The Jetsons". En.Wikipedia.Org, 2018, https://en.wikipedia.org/wiki/The_Jetsons
— "Ruby". En.Wikipedia.Org, 2018, https://en.wikipedia.org/wiki/Ruby.
— "Rubies Are Rare And Precious Gemstones With A Rich And Brilliant Red Colouring". Miningoilgasjobs.Com.Au, 2018

ABOUT DELORISE

DeLorise Simmons (Toots), 66, of New Haven, Connecticut, was born on November 13, 1942 in West Virginia and restored back to her original form on Thursday, December 4, 2008, after a long illness.

DeLorise retired in 1997, after 23 years of employment with the State of Connecticut, Department of Social Services. She began her career in the Food Stamp Unit and was afforded what she felt was an opportunity of a lifetime to spearhead the Job Connection Unit. DeLorise then transferred to the Case Maintenance Unit, and thereafter, the Energy Program. Following her retirement from the State of Connecticut, she volunteered at the Yale-New Haven Hospital Diabetic Clinic.

In addition to volunteering, she worked at the Battered Women's Shelter. It was at the shelter that she enjoyed and took pride in mentoring and assisting the residents that were experiencing a difficult season in their lives. DeLorise was an inspiration to many women and would often remind them that they can be and can do anything they put their minds to and take care of themselves in the process.

DeLorise had a God-given gift. She loved to decorate people, places, and things in a manner that was admired by many. DeLorise will be fondly remembered that even in the midst of her illness, she maintained charisma, a style of excellence, and praise in her mouth about the goodness of God.

ABOUT THE AUTHOR

Sheri Powell and her husband Anthony reside in Florida. They have five adult children, three precious grandchildren, and a bouquet of family and friends.

Sheri has an all-embracing journey of volunteering and mentorship with inner-city children, youth ministry, the Boys & Girls Club, and various women's groups.

Sheri lives to encourage women of all ages that every season of their life has a purpose.

Though Sheri possesses a Bachelor's degree in Church Ministry and an Associate of Arts in Christian Counseling, she does not let degrees or titles define her. God has given her a slideshow of her life. In it, the Spirit of the Lord God is upon her, and the LORD has anointed her to preach good tidings unto the meek. He is sending her to bind up the brokenhearted, to proclaim liberty to the captives, to open the prison to them who are bound…and to comfort all who mourn (Isaiah 61:1-3 & Luke 4:18-19).

Sheri has other selections: *Pausing With God: A Journey Through Menopause* (English & Spanish versions) and *Pausing With God: A Shut In Experience*. She lives and breathes to simply do God's will. With an inherent desire to "Share the Lord with People," Sheri founded and created the SLP Company. Its goal is to share available resources that can help willing participants be all that God has created them to be. Sheri looks forward to watching God show up and show His creation that He is who He says He is and will do what He has said He will do.

If you have a story or comments to share, email us at: PausingWithGod@gmail.com or write us at: Sheri Powell C/O SLP Company P. O. Box 9172 Fleming Isle, FL 32006

www.ingramcontent.com/pod-product-compliance
Lightning Source LLC
Chambersburg PA
CBHW071414290426
44108CB00014B/1816